CHRIS

THE CATERPILLAR AND FRIENDS

BY J T SCOTT

CHRIS

THE CATERPILLAR AND FRIENDS
BY J T SCOTT

Bumper the Bumblebee

Boris the Butterfly

Chris the Caterpillar

William and Wendy the Worms

Sally the Sparrow

Kirsty the Kitten

The Three Fish

Gertrude the Gnome

It was a very special day in the garden.

Chris the Caterpillar

was celebrating his birthday!

"You'll have to wait and see,"

said the Queen Bumblebee.

"Why don't you ask **Bumper the Bumblebee?**

You could ask him if he is free."

"Hello Bumper," said Chris.

"Are you coming to my birthday party?

I have invited all my friends."

"I don't know yet," said Bumper.

"I am busy making lots of balloons.

Maybe I will see you later today."

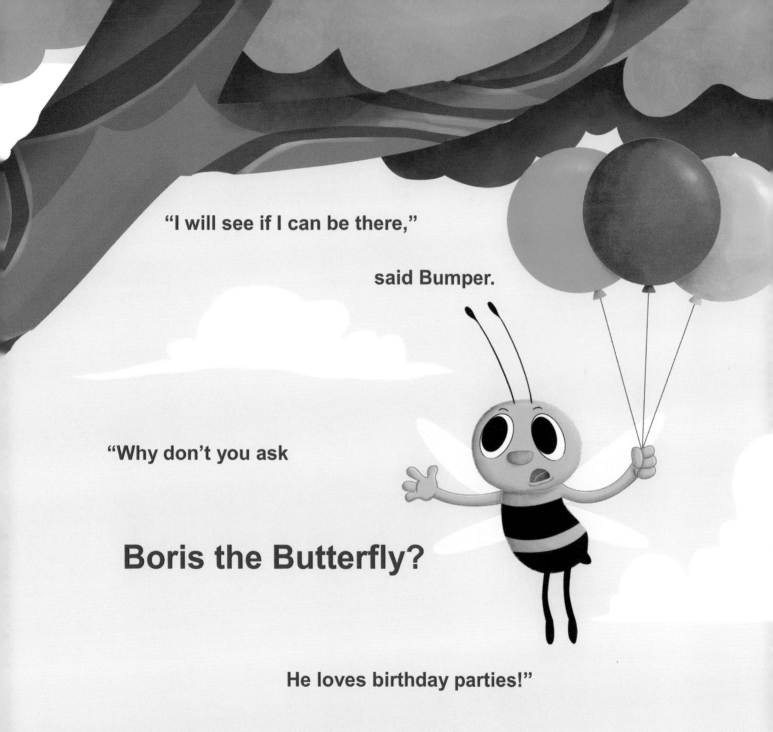

"I will see if I can be there,"

said Bumper.

"Why don't you ask

Boris the Butterfly?

He loves birthday parties!"

Loud music was coming from inside Boris's house.

"Hello Boris," said Chris.

"Are you coming to my birthday party?

I have invited all my friends."

"Thank you for inviting me," said Boris.

"I am learning to play musical instruments.

Would you like me to play you a song?"

"It's my birthday today," said Chris.

"Please can you play a birthday song

and I will sing along?"

"I need to practice so I can play in tune," said Boris.

"Maybe I will see you later on.

Why don't you visit

William and Wendy the Worms

perhaps they can come to your party?"

"Hello William, hello Wendy," said Chris.

"Are you coming to my birthday party?

I sent you an invitation last week."

"We are busy making cakes," said William.

"We love cakes and have lots of cakes to bake," said Wendy.

"Maybe we will see you later today."

"It's my birthday," said Chris.

"I'm having a birthday party

and I'd like all my friends to come along."

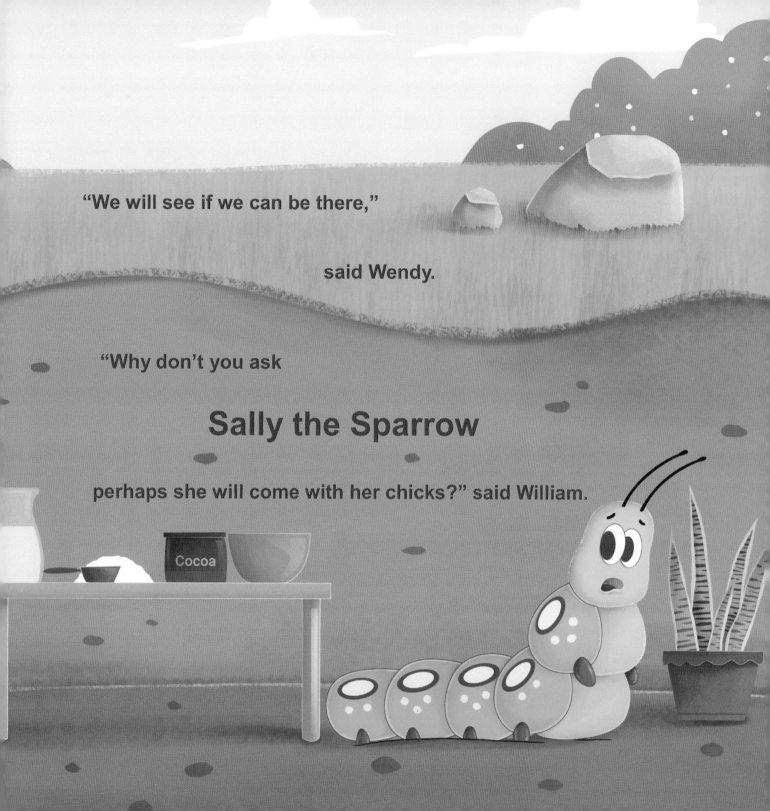

"We will see if we can be there,"

said Wendy.

"Why don't you ask

Sally the Sparrow

perhaps she will come with her chicks?" said William.

"Hello Sally" said Chris.

"Are you coming to my birthday party?

I have invited everyone and your chicks can come too!"

"I am teaching my chicks to play games," said Sally.

"We like playing games.

Do you want to play games with us today?"

"It's my birthday," said Chris.

"I'm having a birthday party

and I'd like all my friends to come along."

"We will see if we can be there,"

said Sally.

"Why don't you ask

Kirsty the Kitten

perhaps she is able to come to your party?"

"Hello Kirsty" said Chris.

"Are you coming to my birthday party?

Everyone seems very busy today.

I hope you can come to my party."

"My friends have come to visit," said Kirsty.

"We are making bunting decorations.

Maybe we will see you tomorrow instead."

"But it's my birthday today," said Chris.

"I'm having a special birthday party

and I'd like all my friends to come along."

"I will see if I can be there,"

said Kirsty.

"Why don't you ask

The Three Fish

perhaps they would like to celebrate with you?"

"Hello fish" said Chris.

"Did you know that it is my birthday today?

Would you like to come to my party?"

"We are busy blowing big bubbles," said one of the fish.

"We will blow some big birthday bubbles for you!"

"But it's my birthday today," said Chris.

"I'm trying to have a special birthday party

and no one seems to want to come along."

"When we have finished blowing big bubbles

we will see if we can come to your party,"

said the fish.

"Why don't you ask

Gertrude the Gnome?

She knows everything there is to know about birthday parties."

"Hello Gertrude," said Chris.

"Did you know it is my birthday today?

I wanted to have a birthday party

with my friends,

but they are all busy

doing other things."

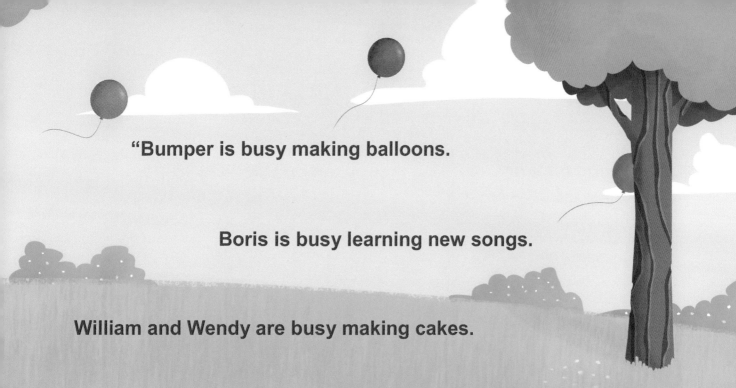

"Bumper is busy making balloons.

Boris is busy learning new songs.

William and Wendy are busy making cakes.

Sally is busy playing games with her chicks.

Kirsty is busy making bunting decorations with her friends.

The Three Fish are busy blowing big bubbles.

It's my birthday and I haven't got any friends to come to my party."

"Your friends are not as busy as they seem," said Gertrude.

"They have been arranging a surprise party for you.

This will be your last birthday as a caterpillar.

Tomorrow you will become a butterfly like Boris!"

"I will become a butterfly!"

said Chris.

"I will change from a caterpillar

shuffling on the ground

into a beautiful butterfly

fluttering around!

That is a very exciting birthday present!"

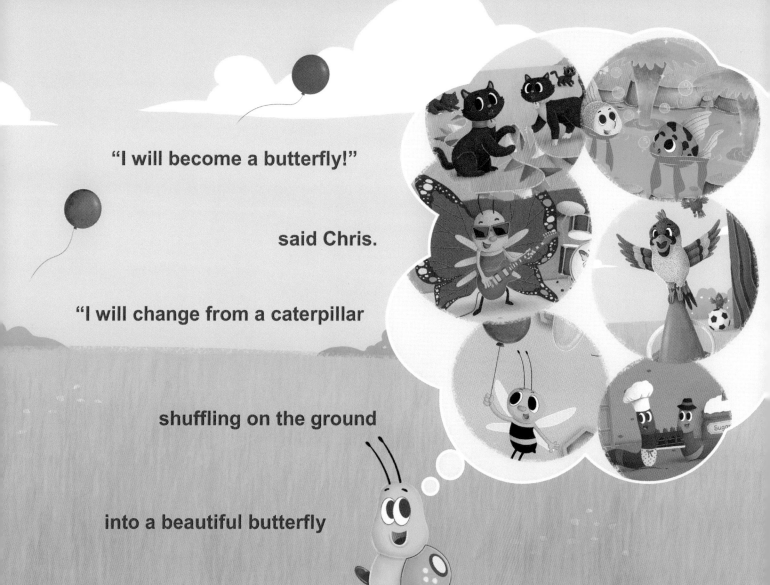

"Thank you for coming to my party!" said Chris.

"This is the best birthday I have ever had!"

CHRIS

THE CATERPILLAR AND FRIENDS

BY J T SCOTT

Chris the Caterpillar and Friends is dedicated to Mum & D2.

J T SCOTT

J T Scott lives in Cornwall surrounded by open countryside,
lots of castles, pens, paper and a vivid imagination.

She has also written the Sammy Rambles series
and created the inclusive game Dragonball Sport.

Sammy Rambles and the Floating Circus
Sammy Rambles and the Land of the Pharaohs
Sammy Rambles and the Angel of 'El Horidore
Sammy Rambles and the Fires of Karmandor
Sammy Rambles and the Knights of the Stone Cross

www.sammyrambles.com
www.dragonball.uk.com

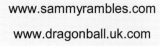

Printed in Poland
by Amazon Fulfillment
Poland Sp. z o.o., Wrocław